Life Coaching

George Edwards

Oval Books

Published by Oval Books
5 St John's Buildings
Canterbury Crescent
London SW9 7QH
United Kingdom

Telephone: +44 (0)20 7582 7123
Fax: +44 (0)20 7582 1022
E-mail: info@ovalbooks.com
Web site: ovalbooks.com

Series Editor – Anne Tauté

Cover designer – Vicki Towers
Printer – J. H. Haynes & Co Ltd., Sparkford
Producer – Oval Projects Ltd.

Cover image – © Stone/Getty Images

The Bluffer's® Guides series is based
on an original idea by Peter Wolfe.

ISBN-13: 978-1-906042-13-4
ISBN-10: 1-906042-13-6

CONTENTS

THE DOs AND DON'TS

What life coaches don't do

Life coaching is a very strange beast in the personal growth jungle, in that its practitioners invariably seem to be more concerned to make it clear what they don't do, than to explain what they do. This is very effective at limiting criticism and reducing any potential for blaming them for interventions that don't work out as expected. If coaches don't actually claim to do something, they can't be blamed for doing it badly. Or not doing it at all.

Most life coaches will start their proposition by telling you that life coaching is not about therapy. It is really important to them that you should know it

> **66 Practitioners invariably seem to be more concerned to make it clear what they don't do, than to explain what they do. 99**

isn't about therapy. Even if you don't know what therapy is, it is probable that you will have heard about it and it has, to be fair, had a mixed press.

An essential then for any bluffer on first hearing the words 'life coaching' is to look thoughtfully at the speaker, and then at a suitable moment to interject, "Of course, it's really important to separate life coaching from therapy." This will have been drummed into the coachee or potential

1

coachee so thoroughly that it will immediately mark the bluffer as a fellow enthusiast and one who knows. A sage nod after the coachee's response can be followed up with "A mistake so many people make, of course!" which will put the seal of certainty on one's expert status.

In fact the real bluff is that there shouldn't be many people who make this mistake since almost every source of information on life coaching, from the smallest leaflet to the thickest self-help book will make it clear that the two are not remotely related.

> **❝ Every source of information will make it clear that life coaching and therapy are not remotely related. ❞**

You can explain that the essential differences between life coaching and therapy are the 'time frame of the intervention, the purpose, and the relationship between the practitioner and coachee'. What is meant here is that the therapist is largely concerned with the consequences of past experiences that their patients have already suffered, and helping them to recover or come to terms with them. The therapy supposition is that the past is messing up the present and therefore the future. A lot of psychological therapy centres on what the poet Philip Larkin referred to in his famous couplet, 'They fuck you up, your mum and dad', which gives endless vicarious excitement to therapy as a profession.

So to the therapist for a patient to get to the future he/she wants the past needs to be exposed (bleeding and pulsing) and dealt with under the stern gaze of the therapist. The strength coachees gain from this experience is supposed to enable them to put aside the problems they have been carrying around on their backs, distorting their lives.

Life coaching on the other hand is not about the past. It works on the assumption that what you make of your life is up to you. Coachees need to take careful note of this, for it is the main term and condition in every life coaching agreement. In short, success is up to the coachee to address here and now, the coachee has the answers, and the coachee needs to make his or her own changes.

> **66 Life coaching works on the assumption that what you make of your life is up to you. Take careful note of this, for it is the main term and condition in every life coaching agreement. 99**

Having negotiated the smooth waters of what coaching isn't, it is safe for you to venture a view that life coaching is a very existentialist phenomenon. If puzzled eyebrows are raised, a terse and confident summary of the existentialist theory as it applies to life coaching will suffice, as follows. "Existentialism holds that everyone has complete freedom to make their own decisions, and is responsible for the outcomes of those decisions. This produces 'angst', and it is this 'anxiety' or 'anguish' that the coaching process focuses on. This acts as a force to produce desired change and a fuller potential in the coachee's life. It's really quite obvious if you think about it, isn't it?"

Few listeners will be in a position to challenge the bluffer on this final question tag, and a challenge would in any case be no threat for in an existential way challengers would have to bear the consequences of their decision to argue with an obvious expert. "Game," as they say, "set and match" to you.

> **66 It is 'angst' that the coaching process focuses on to produce desired change in the coachee's life. 99**

It may be that a particularly slow interlocutor confuses therapy with psychiatry. If so, it is enough to wearily point out that psychiatry is a medical specialisation concerned with the diagnosis and treatment of disorders that have primarily mental or behavioural symptoms. As a clincher, the bluffer will add "That's why life coaches don't have patients!"

* There is a top class bluffer-led discussion to be gained from the names given to the subject of coaching. In mentoring terminology, the classical term is 'protégé', but it's a bit fuddy-duddy for life coaching. 'Learner' isn't quite right either, and 'patient', for reasons that will be spelled out, is entirely inappropriate. So 'coachee' it is.

4

before moving purposely to the buffet or bar.

The advantage of this strategy is that not only will it not only show deep understanding and erudition, but it will hold the door open to anyone present who either practices as a life coach or has some experience of the process. They are almost certain to leap in with a tale of regularly disabusing their coachees of this notion or, if a coachee, of how their own coach explained the differences. It is pretty much a certainty that a coachee will have had this particular explanation. As has been pointed out, life coaches establish very early on what they don't do, even if they leave what they do do as a bit of a mystery.

> **66 Life coaches establish very early on what they don't do, even if they leave what they do do as a bit of a mystery. 99**

What life coaches do

Anyone who has found and visited a dentist in the last few years, one that is who can be afforded without a platinum credit card or a large inheritance, will have noticed the change that has come over the dental profession of late. As you lie back in a steel and vinyl throne under the high power lamps, pink water in the fountain gurgling to your left, waiting for the injection to take effect, it is likely that the dentist will be telling you what he is going to do.

You see, the bluffer will point out patiently, most of the high street professions – 'professions' intoned with a knowing emphasis, to indicate that certain of what used to be called the professions, for example dentists, opticians, accountants, who now trade on the high streets, like, well, like tradesmen – are now aware that their customers deserve to know what they are getting for their money, what exactly they do, that justifies the fees.

This is why the solicitor will explain what she is going to do for you, rather than simply saying, in a Dickensian manner, 'Don't fret, Old Chap, Leave it all to Sploggs and Sploggs, for I assure you, you have engaged the best there is in this town, indeed— don't forget your hat— and this is the address for the, er, account.'

> **The essential proposition (bluffers love 'essential propositions' and treat them with reverence), is that the coach won't do anything for you. Or to you.**

And the accountants will wrinkle their brows and explain why IR35 is such an interesting set of requirements, and how they will have to perform certain fiscal miracles that only the true professional understands in order to maintain the basic promise that an accountant should cost you less than they save you.

But the Life Coach now, the life coach, brave new profession that it is, has something of a difficulty in using this patter, in telling the client what exactly

6

they are going to do for them to explain their entitlement to fees. Because the essential proposition (bluffers love 'essential propositions', and treat them with reverence), the essential proposition is that the coach won't do anything for you. Or to you.

Unlike the accountant, who acts as intermediary between you and the blood-sucking leeches of taxation, the coach will only act as an intermediary between you as coachee and, (not to put to fine a point on it) yourself. There is no third party involved. The coach will not write letters for you. The coach will not intervene on behalf of you. The coach will not even, dentist-like, advise you to forsake certain habits.

> **The coach will help the coachee to make a more functional, satisfying relationship with the monkey, and then cheerfully wave the pair of them out of the door.**

So what will the coach do? The coach will enable the coachees to do things for themselves. It's a golden rule. When the future coachee arrives with the proverbial monkey on his back, the coach will encourage his potential customer to describe the monkey, will listen carefully to this, and then ask what, if anything, the person on the chair opposite wishes to do about the monkey. The coach will help the coachee to make a more functional, satisfying relationship with the monkey, and then cheerfully wave the pair of them out of the door (by way of reception) either still in a bottom-to-shoulder relationship, or possibly by then hand in hand, or even one pursued by the other, hopefully with the human to the rear.

You see, the life coach won't actually do anything, in the sense of 'doing' that many professionals recognise. At no time will the life coach suggest a strategy for unseating the monkey, or physically remove the simian difficulty. No practical advice relating to the mechanics of monkey removal will be proffered. The life coach does not advertise as 'Ex-Simian Ltd, the Monkey Removal Specialists'. The monkey and all aspects of its management remains the absolute and exclusive property of the coachee.

> **66 At no time will the life coach suggest a strategy for unseating the monkey, or physically remove the simian difficulty. 99**

Now clearly it isn't an attractive proposition or particularly marketable for life coaches to approach potential coachees on the basis that they are not going to actually, how shall we put it, *do* anything. So coaches have a patter to disguise this absence of any real intervention. It's called 'The journey'. And what they do is help the coachees on their journey. The journey starts with what can be called 'discovery'.

How life coaches do what they do

'Discovery' is the process of uncovering where the future coachee now is. Or where they feel they are. Or what they feel unhappy about. Or what is irritating them. Or what they want to fix. Sometimes they call this the present, the here-and-now. Sometimes they may call it the 'starting point'. The life coach will devote the first session or the first couple of sessions, to getting the new customer to describe the starting point of their journey in their own words, to clarify

> 66 Coaches will share with their coachees just enough to convince them there are arcane secrets, worth paying for. 99

what exactly is causing them difficulties and has brought them to take that very sensible first step over the life coaches welcoming threshold. Coaches have a favourite bit of jargon they will share with their coachees for any combination of circumstances that have brought them to the arrangement; they call these 'Life events'.

At this point the bluffer will give a chuckle, and point out that all professions have two types of jargon:

1 the terms they will share with a coachee so that they are let into the arcane secrets just enough to convince them there are arcane secrets, worth paying for;

9

2 the terms that are kept entirely secret, such as the doctor's 'LOBNH' (Lights On But Nobody Home).

'Life events' are almost anything that happens to people in the modern world with the effect of causing a bit of angst or stress. The big ones tend to be marriage, divorce, children, no children, new job, loss of job, illness, someone else's illness, managing time, moving to a new place, staying in one place. You get the idea. 'Limited' is not really the right the word to apply to life events.

❝ Life events provide ample reasons for seeking the assistance of a life coach before getting to the point of attacking the car windscreen. ❞

As they are cumulative, life events provide ample reasons for seeking the assistance of a life coach in reorganising one's 'journey' before getting to the point of attacking the car windscreen with a branch torn from a convenient suburban tree, or retreating into the happy embrace of international distilling or pharmaceutical corporations.

So the discovery process almost inevitably starts with an outpouring of life events by the new customer. These are not going to be particularly useful to the life coach as he or she starts from the premise that 'that was then and this is now', and that the important thing is not the past but the present and the journey to the future. The coach, our wise old bluffer will remind us, is not a therapist, and does not subscribe to the theory that in the past lies the key to the future.

As the life events come pouring forth, it is vital that the coach doesn't interrupt, or even worse, voice an opinion or give advice. The coach has to be almost obsessive about this passivity. When the coachee explains how he had to take a chain saw to the car of a relative, or reduce his brother in law's shed to a pile of kindling, and asks, innocently, 'Well, I didn't really have any alternative, did I?', the life coach will not nod, will not agree, will not sympathise.

Instead, the practised life coach will respond with, "And that's what you felt you had to do, is it?" This cunning strategy, so beloved of politicians, consists of always responding to a question with another question. So, the indirect, "Do you see what I mean?" is met with, "Would you like me to?", and the indirect plea for sympathy met with "Is that what you want for yourself?"

❝At this point life coaches will be subliminally training their coachees not to expect any solutions to be provided.❞

The object of discovery therefore is not to provide any solutions, indeed at this point life coaches will be subliminally training their coachees not to expect any solutions to be provided. The real point of the discovery process is to get coachees to adequately explain their current position, for from it springs that essential expression of dissatisfaction with their lot.

Gently, perhaps even firmly, establishing this dissatisfaction is vital. It is dissatisfaction that causes angst. At this point it is opportune for the bluffer to remind the audience that "Angst" is not a useful term to share with a coachee, even if Angst is not strictly (it is a good idea to acknowledge this distinction) "jargon". 'Angst' expresses the dread reality that the coachee's present is unsatisfactory, and their future unknown, and that as a result the choices that they make are the sole determining factor in their future happiness. As the Chinese proverb has it (one of many obscure Chinese proverbs that are of considerable value to the life coach, because they only really make sense to the recipient well after the session has ended: 'If you don't change the direction you are travelling in, you are going to arrive at where you're going.'

> **❝As the Chinese proverb has it: 'If you don't change the direction you are travelling in, you are going to arrive at where you're going.'❞**

Only when the discovery process has been fully aired, and in itself acted to an extent like the valve on a pressure cooker, enabling a release of steam, and through this simple mechanism already making the coachee feel less pressurised and generally more content, will the life coach feel it is time to move on to the options available to deal with their dissatisfaction. Or to be more precise, only then will the coach feel it is time to help coachees themselves move on to an inspection of the options available to deal with their dissatisfaction.

> **66 Only when the discovery process has been fully aired, will the life coach feel it is time to move on. 99**

This huge responsibility for their own future, how to determine it, what it will look like, and how to achieve it, drives the coachee back to the life coach session after session to pour out their thoughts, dreams and plans, for truly (and happily), life coaching is a 'talking cure'.

THE ORIGINS OF LIFE COACHING

The term 'Coaching' was first used in its modern sense to refer to the person who trains athletes or sports players some time around 1889. Before that there is some evidence that the word had been used, as it can be today, for a tutor or teacher working privately for a family or individual. The bluffer can score by pointing out that, in the case of coaching in general, far from the world adopting a sporting term, which is the usual direction, sport has adopted a word that others were using first.

An extra gloss of erudition is gained from an instructive verbal footnote to the effect that the word 'coach' is said to be derived from the town of Kosice [pronounced 'co-see-chay'] in Slovakia, where that form of conveyance was supposedly invented. Even today 'coach' is used as another name for a bus, and – this is the really clever bit – a coach takes you from where you are to somewhere new. You may permit yourself a small, superior smile here as you suggest with suitable gravitas that coaching today is still essentially about taking you to a new place in your life.

> **66 Far from the world adopting a sporting term, which is the usual direction, sport has adopted a word that others were using first. 99**

A Californian hybrid

Personal or life coaching is claimed to have begun in California in the early 1980s, when one Thomas Leonard, an accountant, realised that many of his clients were looking for more than just financial advice.

By 1985 the term 'executive coaching' was in use for Leadership Development programmes in

California, and soon afterwards the term 'coaching' had become sufficiently mainstream for *Forbes* magazine, a favoured magazine of wealthy American corporate executives, to run a (possibly derisive) article entitled, 'Sigmund Freud meets Henry Ford'. This described executive coaching as a controversial hybrid of management consulting and psychotherapy, which is essentially about taking something that few people understand and making it into a mass market product for people who don't know how it works. That analysis is one which the life coaching industry has ever since been trying to sweep away.

Even in the US it took a while for the 'personal' or 'life coach' to appear, and the transmutation of the American original into other cultural versions took a few more years. However, within 15 years the term life coach had taken root in Europe,

66 The article described executive coaching as a controversial hybrid of management consulting and psychotherapy... an analysis that the life coaching industry has ever since been trying to sweep away. 99

Australia, New Zealand, and parts of Asia, and its proponents were celebrating its status as 'the second fastest growing profession'. Second fastest by what criterion was (if not hard to say) at least better left unsaid, but it had certainly begun to creep up the employment league tables past computer software engineers and dental assistants.

An established perennial

Today personal coaching is a regular part of executive outplacement packages, and many organisations also provide an element of life coaching as part of their employee support programmes. There are two sides to espouse, both favourable:

1 The worldly-wise commentator will take the line that for such employers there is the inestimable benefit that the process may convince the unwanted employee that the thing they really want to do anyway is to cease being an executive transport consigner and become a self-employed tofu farmer. This enables the coachee to depart with both a redundancy cheque and a happy smile.

2 Others may believe that it is a lack of personal focus that prevents maximum executive performance, and feel that a small expenditure on coaching support is cheaper than initiating a separation process with their under-

performing employee and re-advertising the position.

As coaching now establishes itself firmly outside the corporate world, it develops a whole range of new advantage and benefit propositions which range from dealing with teenagers, to finding inner peace. Apostles of life coaching will point out that everybody has something they would like 'fixed', even if it's something that without benefit of alcohol and 'intimac', they might not choose to share with the wider world.

> **66** Apostles of life coaching will point out that everybody has something they would like 'fixed'. **99**

THE LIFE COACH'S TOOLBAG

It will have become apparent that for the life coaches there are really only two skills, only two clubs in their golf bag, only two tools in their toolbox:

1 one is the ability to seem to listen without nodding off or getting trapped into offering sympathy, advice, or opinion (see 'Empathy'.)

2 the other is the ability to ask a lot of questions.

Questions

As any coachee is likely to know, or be able to work out after a few sessions with their life coach, there are only really two types of questions. With only two skills, and one of those only in two alternatives, the life coach's cupboard seems remarkably bare.

❝The purpose of a question asked by a life coach is not to find the answer. It is to help the coachee find the answer.❞

Naturally, it isn't quite that simple, because just as to the casual drinker one beer mat looks rather the same as another, to a tegestologist (–look, this is a guide about Life Coaching, Oh all right then, beer mat collector–) each is unique, and each has a special purpose, a distinct character, and a virtue of its own. So to the skilled life coach, it is the purpose of the question that differentiates their myriad virtues.

So starting from the premise that there are only really two types of question –

- the 'closed question' which leads to a choice of 'Yes', 'No', or 'I don't know', and
- the open question, beginning with one of Kipling's famous 'serving men' – What, When, Why, etc., each of which will elicit from the one being questioned a detailed answer,

the life coach works on the purpose of the questions. The purpose of a question asked by a life coach is not to find the answer. It is to help the coachee find the answer.

As the artist Yves Klein said – admittedly only of his International Klein Blue paintings* – a single simple object can also have 'values beyond what can be seen or touched'. This is the real skill of the life coach. An ever so simple, basic question, can have a vast range of purposes. Consider if you will, these five questions:

1 "And **why** didn't you do anything about it earlier?"
2 "And why **didn't** you do anything about it earlier?"
3 "And why didn't **you** do anything about it earlier?"
4 "And why didn't you do **any**thing about it earlier?"
5 "And why didn't you do anything about it **earlier**?"

Here you see the extraordinary subtlety of the full range of questions available to the life coach. Although seemingly so simple to answer, they will reveal a vast hinterland of concerns, limiting beliefs, excuses, and stresses. In order, the responses may uncover – for these are 'uncovering questions':

---

* in which the colour (in this case, blue) effectively becomes the art

- Because I was simply too busy
- Because I didn't think it mattered
- Because I didn't think it was up to him/her any-way
- Because I decided it was hopeless
- Because I thought it would go away if left alone.

All of which open up the discussion, and enable the coach to take the coachee further down the path of discovery, to strip away the layers of excuse, prevarication, despair, and fatalism, and begin to recognise the reality of his/her current position.

66 The feedback will follow a pattern, well-established as the 'feedback sandwich', which is one of those pieces of jargon the life coach will not be sharing. 99

Naturally, this activity can't be allowed to lead to a situation where coachees become so depressed that quaffing hemlock is seen as the most obvious solution to their plight. If that were the case life coaches would be very short of customers, and they aren't. So the life coach must always have a way of dealing with the negatives that pour forth. This is where feedback comes to their assistance.

Feedback is, as the bluffer will point out, a mechanism by which coachees can be encouraged to learn from what they have revealed about their life events and their reactions to them. So at the end of session one, the feedback will follow a well-established pattern, known as the 'feedback sandwich', which is one of those pieces of jargon the life coach will not be sharing. The feedback sandwich for this particular coachee may go like this:

1 (**Top slice**) "Well, it's time for us to wrap things up for this session. First of all, you must feel very pleased with yourself that you have decided you need to take things in hand, and deal with them. That's good, a very hopeful sign for the future, so well done."

2 (**Filling**) "Of course, there are some serious difficulties you have uncovered today; your loathing for your entire family, your alcoholism, the suicidal tendencies, the drug taking and the obsessive scratching."

3 (**Bottom slice**) "But there is so much positive that has come out of today as well. You have begun to understand why you have these feelings, and to address the effect that the behaviours have on you, and you've started to work out that there may be an alternative. That's very positive, and next time we meet we can decide to go forward on that journey towards the life you really want!"

With that, the bluffer will close up the small triangular brown bread and ham sandwich that has served as a focal point for the explanation about giving useful feedback to their small but enthralled audience. And eat it.

Empathy

Life coaches are big on empathy. Tell your life coach your cat has died, and like as not you'll get no sympathy, but you will get lashings of empathy.

The difference between sympathy and empathy is one of those distinctions that the bluffer is so good at. On announcing that empathy has to be one of the life coaches skills, the bluffer will be ready for the obvious question with a witty riposte. In this case, the feline fatality already mentioned forms a vehicle. Sympathy is when in this situation the coach can say, "I imagine it must be dreadful to lose a cat", whereas empathy is, "I know just how it feels to lose a cat." Which is almost a perfect separation of the two concepts. Or to put it more succinctly, empathy involves understanding the other's position, and sympathy involves having compassion for it. Life coaches

> **❝Life coaches are big on empathy. Tell your life coach your cat has died, and like as not you'll get no sympathy, but you will get lashings of empathy. ❞**

don't do professional compassion. They do empathy instead. And to do empathy requires a degree of worldliness, a wealth of experience, and an understanding of where the other person is standing.

This can be difficult for you as a life coach – if indeed you are intending to become a life coach – because you can't really have had all the same experiences as everyone who walks into your sessions. So you may have to fabricate empathy. Quite often.

Life coaches do this by concentrating on feelings. Not their feelings as life coaches, that would get in the way of the empathising.

> **66 Once the killer question has been asked, "How do you feel about that?", life coaches have a nail on which to hang their empathy. 99**

One needs a clear head for empathising. So the life coach has to develop ways of creating empathy. As Groucho Marx might have put it, "Now I can fake feelings, I can fake anything."

Feelings fall into some pretty definite categories. For example, there's sad, there's angry, there's helpless, there's pleased. This is the key to fake empathy. Once the killer question – incidentally one that therapists and even psychiatrists are not above using for their own purposes – has been asked, "How do you feel about that?", life coaches have a nail on which to hang their empathy.

If the response is 'sad' or a synonym of sad, or a

moderation of sad, coaches can go quickly through the database of their own experiences, and come upon 'sad'. Of course, for the coach it may be his 'sad' is how he felt when discovering who had really drunk that good bottle of sherry on Christmas eve, while to the coachee 'sad' may be the loss of the only job that mattered, but both can tune into 'sad'. So with this feeling in mind, rather than the coachee's specific context for the feeling, it is perfectly possible for the coach to fabricate empathy.

> **❝ Practising detachment and the skilful use of empathy is a primary life coaching skill. ❞**

All of which is, the bluffer will add, can seem a bit hard on life coaches. Some do come from long and interesting careers before opting for the life of a coach, and may genuinely understand the feelings of their coachees. However, even for these superhumans, it is dangerous to get into the causes of the feelings too deeply. True, a near identical experience may have befallen the life coach, but that is not the point. The point is what has befallen the coachee. Practising detachment and the skilful use of empathy is a primary life coaching skill, and like all life skills, even the initiated bluffer can get it wrong.

There are, however, a few absolutely copperbottomed, dead cert., can't lose at any price, ways to ruin empathy.

1 Interpretation

The first absolute disaster is the stereotype response, typified by, 'So, what you're trying to say is.....'

> **66 Interpretation is the coachee's job, along with everything else in the life coaching relationship. 99**

When coachees express a feeling or opinion, it is their feeling or opinion. The life coach must on no account attempt to classify it for them. The coachee isn't trying to say anything that the coach can supply an interpretation for; interpretation is the coachee's job, along with everything else in the life coaching relationship.

2 Inattention

Next in the list of crimes against empathy is, 'Yes, really? Oh me, oh dear!' said in that way that very quickly makes even the thickest skinned coachee realise that the coach is thinking about the road tax on the car and wondering if the cheque is actually in the envelope, or if forgotten in a 'must check before posting, I wonder if I have any stamps' sort of way. The coachee is paying for undivided empathy, and will soon notice this one.

3 Theorising

Next comes telling coachees what they mean, possibly using theories out of The Big Book of

Life Coaching, saying for instance: 'Your response is very typical of a crossed transaction between natural child and nurturing parent', or some such popular psychological theory. It isn't. It's very typical of the way the coachee typically thinks and feels at that typical moment.

4 Long-windedness

Almost as bad as attempting to tell coachees why they feel the way they do is explaining why you, the life coach, are able to empathise. The coachee is not shelling out oodles of dosh per hour to listen to the life coach's own life stories.

5 Looking for a meaning

And last, possibly the nub of more therapist jokes than anyone has ever heard, usually with 'How do you feel about that?' in them, is the psychological game. This involves looking for a meaning behind everything. So a quick look at the clock on the wall is met with 'Why are you worried about the time?', and a request to draw the curtains with 'Does sunlight bother you?'

66 The coachee is not shelling out oodles of dosh to listen to the life coach's own life stories. 99

Life coaches need to be aware that not everything has a significance, and they shouldn't try to find any. A bit like *Big Brother*.

All in all, empathy is a tricky game, but as Groucho Marx might also have put it, had the word been in use at the time, 'Once I could fake empathy, I could really sympathise with anyone.'

LIFE COACHES AND LIFE EVENTS

Beliefs

Life coaches keep their own beliefs pretty much to themselves. You won't catch a life coach saying, "I believe" very often, unless it's followed by "...I'm seeing you again next Tuesday" or "we've made a lot of progress". They will shy away from anything that to the coachee smacks of a personal conviction or belief, on the grounds that (as any experienced bluffer will remind listeners in world weary tone), it's the coachee's belief that counts. Life coaches however regard belief as the sort of thing their anyone has a right to, as long as it is the right sort of belief, the sort of belief that the coachee wants. And importantly, a belief that the coachee needs.

> **❝ You won't catch a life coach saying, "I believe" very often, unless it's followed by "...I'm seeing you again next Tuesday". ❞**

In fact, life coaches are pretty hot on helping coachees to decide what beliefs they want and what they need. To do this they employ the practice so beloved of police dramas, which in that case is called 'Good cop – Bad cop' and, as we know, always produces a result the police want, only in the case of life coaches, it's 'Good Belief – Bad Belief'.

> **A coachee who leaves the room skipping and singing 'I believe I can fly' will at least make some positive changes in the general direction of achieving it.**

A 'good belief' is what the life coach helps the coachee to discover is 'an enabling belief', and a bad belief is what the coachee has to realise is a 'limiting belief'. The coachee has to realise this, not be told it, or not be told it until they have stumbled on it and are seeking for words to describe one of these nasty, undesirable beliefs, in which case the life coach may well come to the rescue with a useful aside of, "that's what we call a limiting belief", using 'we' as the royal 'We', and not as the professional 'we' meaning 'the two of us', so prevalent in the medical profession ('How are we feeling today?'). Unless the life coach is trying to make a point about how professional he or she is, which is the coach's enabling belief.

A good belief to the life coach is one that spurs the coachee on to greater, or at least different

28

efforts. So coachees who have a goal, need to believe they can achieve the goal. For belief (the bluffer will sagely point out to the debutante here) is self-reinforcing. A coachee who leaves the room skipping along and singing 'I believe I can fly' may not actually achieve that feat, but will at least make some positive changes in the general direction of achieving it. And those little changes produce small successes, which reinforce a general feeling of being able to do things.

Limiting beliefs

On the other hand, the "Bad Cop" side of beliefs are what the life coach will refer to, if it is already established that the coachee has identified them, as 'limiting beliefs'. Limiting beliefs are all the baggage coachees carry around with them that effectively stop them achieving what they have decided they need to achieve.

> **Limiting beliefs are all the baggage coachees carry around with them that actually stop them achieving what they have decided they need to achieve.**

Limiting beliefs tend to start with an expression like 'I can't' or 'I couldn't', and go on to identify what the coachee actually knows full well is a necessary step towards his or her own salvation. So 'But I could never tell my father-in-law to get lost!' is an expression of desire, and need to be followed up (the bluffer may pause here a moment before adding) with huge incisiveness, "Why?" before sitting back while coachees find one after another excuses for not doing what they want to do, and deep down know they should do.

The fact of the matter is that limiting beliefs are usually the result of experience, although the life coach doesn't ever explore the experience that may have created them, as this would be straying into therapy. The coach simply needs to assist the coachee in uncovering these Bad Cop beliefs.

Enabling beliefs

Enabling beliefs are slightly different; they are the result of desire, and the thing about them is that once the coachee explores the possibility that their goals may actually be within reach, they usually create a virtuous cycle of belief, *viz:* experiment, success, and strengthened belief.

> 66 It's that pivotal change from 'Nothing works for me', to 'I can do whatever I damned well feel like!' that is the main challenge. 99

It's the way sales people manage to stay so 'up' in the face of constant put-downs and abuse; they just know they are the greatest sales person on earth, and each success reinforces that belief. A salesperson's failures are nearly

30

always attributed to the dimwittedness of the person being pitched to, a mental attitude shared by advertising executives, door-to-door missionaries and rejected politicians.

For the life coach, it's that pivotal change from the all-too-common mental position of 'Nothing works for me, I'm so unhappy, nothing will ever get better, it's no use even trying' in Eeyor-ish tones, to 'I can do whatever I damned well feel like!' that is the main challenge. From then on for the life coach it should be largely about sitting back and asking thoughtful, supportive, confidence building questions like 'How', 'When' and 'What' as in:

> 66 Life coaches are generally pretty much in favour of health. There are even some that make it a bit of a specialism. 99

"What do you need in order to do that?"

In no time at all coachees will realise that their life coaches, far from being an irritation with all those "Why do you think that?" questions, and their irksome "What is it that you really want?" prodding, are actually their best friends, the sort who would listen to them in the pub, nod wisely at their insight and strategies, and only interrupt to tell them they are jolly clever to have worked it all out so well. This, and the resulting shift of the workload from coach to coachee, is what the bluffer would call "a win-win outcome".

Health

Life coaches are generally pretty much in favour of health. There are even some that make it a bit of a specialism. They try to live exemplary, healthy lives, lives largely made possible only by the stress-free, home-based, flexible-working, coachee-choosing, fee-setting existence they have adopted. Some life coaches may even be seen buying soya cheese in supermarkets, and munching organic brown rice biscuits with strange South African Rooibos tea.

> **Any life coach is likely at some point to start in on exploring your 'healthy lifestyle options'. They are always 'options', after all, and it is up to the coachee to opt in or out of them.**

In dealings with their coachees then, life coaches who touch on health, or even specialise in it, tend to have a rather prescriptive view of what is good for them, and therefore, naturally, what is good for their coachees. True, active prescription does rather run against life coaching's key principle of never actually telling the coachee what to do, but that doesn't stop one from promoting what one sees as a healthy life. As long as it is done subtlely.

This means that the life coach isn't going to open the first session with, "Well, what a porker you are!", but at some point may start exploring your 'healthy lifestyle options'. They are always 'options', after all, so it is up to the one being coached to opt in or out of them.

There are endless ways for coaches to insinuate 'healthy lifestyle options' into their interactions with coachees. A simple greeting of, "How are you feeling today?" can lead into an exploration of the coachee's sleep patterns, and naturally, almost en passant, casually, non-prescriptively, to the matter of caffeine and its detrimental effect on pure, cleansing, de-stressing, sleep.

A few minutes spent talking about the coachee's daily routine leads innocuously and unobtrusively into a conversation which (remarkably) includes the beneficially fibrous effects on the system of a good muesli-rich start to the day, followed by a light, possibly organic lunch, and a sensible attitude to alcohol. Coaches are very keen indeed on 'Alcohol – a sensible approach to'. Or keen on saying that they are.

> **Some non-advice on the way that exercise produces the feel-good endorphin chemicals, is greatly to be recommended to all as a de-stressor.**

Later perhaps, a conversation about the coachee's inability to find 'any time' for themselves, inevitably leads to gently probing, exploratory, helpful, questions about how much daily exercise is taken, and maybe some non-advice on the way that exercise produces the feel-good endorphin chemicals, and is greatly to be recommended to all as a de-stressor.

So your average life coach is pretty red hot on 'healthy lifestyle options'. But fear not. The life coach is not promoting healthy lifestyle options for the sake of healthy lifestyle options. The life coach is not going to be pressure-selling any gym sub-scriptions. Nor trying and convert anyone to veganism. There is no secret store of aloe vera to sell after the session.

> **66 Committed coachees are more likely to maintain the relationship with the person who gave them the impetus to make the small change. 99**

Rather, the preoccupation with healthy life-style options is part of the grand plan, to encourage coachees to take control of their lives. The rationale is clear and simple, and will be ever so persistent-ly pointed out; if they can't even take control of what they do to their bodies they can't really take control of their lives. Can they?

The adoption of 'healthier lifestyle options' is therefore an integral part of the process of creating little victories. The coachee who bounds into the session and confides that he or she has had a caffeine-free week, and comments, 'Do you know, I feel quite lot perkier!', is a committed coachee. Committed coachees are more likely to maintain the relationship with the person who gave them the impetus to make the small change, and staying with the Person Who Gave Them the Impetus to

Successfully Make the Small Change is likely to be a step on the way to making the big change that the p.w.g.t.t.i.t.m.t.s.c is helping them to work out and enact.

Or, a healthy coachee is a happy coachee, and a happy coachee is an advertisement. Not that life coaches are at all cynical. Or manipulative. Not at all. Far from it.

Success

Success is one of those terms life coaches need to be a bit wary of. The problem with success, is that if it is defined too closely, there is a danger that it also defines 'F*A*I*L*U*R*E'. And failure is not something that life coaches want to be associated with in any way. So the trick is to get a definition of success – and here the weary bluffer will point out in a worldly way that "we all know now" this really means getting one's coachee to find a definition of success he or she is happy with, remembering that life coaches don't do the 'giving the answers' thing.

> **❝ Failure is not something that life coaches want to be associated with in any way. So the trick is to get a definition of success. ❞**

Often the life coach will seek an analogy, or metaphor, to help the coachee to tackle the difficult subject of success. The secret of success, it will turn out, is being content to have achieved what is reasonable to achieve in the light of the resources one has, and being able to achieve more success only by gaining additional resources. If coachees can define what success looks like for them, which may range from a trouble-free life and a reasonable standard of living to a yacht moored below their house in Marbella and never having to save left-overs, then they can get on with the process of working out how to achieve this, and so the setting of their goals.

> **" The secret of success, it will turn out, is being content to have achieved what is reasonable to achieve in the light of the resources one has. "**

Setting goals

If success is the vision, then goals are the definition. If the vision is the millionaire lifestyle, the goals have to include making the millions, and the big fat goal of 'making a million' will have, like the fleas on the back of a flea, smaller contributory fleas, or in this case, goals. In the case of the would-be yacht owner, the big 'I wanna make a million' may include 'getting well-paid employment' (it is wiser for the life coach to avoid suggestions that for that particular coachee with that specific goal, the lottery might actually offer better odds, even at 16 million to one against).

The whole business of success and goal setting then is about walking backwards. Once coachees have defined what success looks like to them, they can set the goal or goals for themselves that will deliver it, and as it's pretty unlikely that the big goal will be reached in one fell swoop, they need also to work out a number of contributory goals. Here the life coach will refer to "steps on the ladder" or "places on the way": metaphors are so very useful in effective goal setting.

The clever life coach spends some time each session reviewing goals* and contributory goals because

> **66 Most life coaches don't use the term 'targets' for the basic reason that people aim at targets and largely miss them. 99**

one of the things that must be done at the end of a session is to send the coachee out of the door with an achievable immediate goal to address, something that they must do before the next meeting, all contributing to a sense of urgency (and if not addressed, guilt) which should not expire before the next session.

Such a contributory goal may be as simple as signing up for that conversational Spanish course,

* Most life coaches don't use the term 'targets' for the very basic reason that people aim at targets and largely miss them, but a goal is a goal when it has been scored, even if it's an own goal.

or as major as informing the Aged Relative that there are many housing associations that will offer a far better service than the coachee is able to continue to offer, but a contributory goal before the next session always needs to be something that the coachee can, and therefore probably will, achieve.

Work

Life coaches can find it hard to understand the place of jobs and paid employment in their coachees' lives, perhaps because their own are not standard and therefore not generally considered to be a 'proper job'. The life coach has after all been through that strange transition and the associated decision to let go of 'real work', and become a free-lance sooth-sayer (or as the bluffer would point out, a sooth-listener).

"Your boss is being difficult? Why don't you tell him what you think about that?"

"Your company has demanded you take a pay cut? Why can't you tell them you won't stand for it?"

"Your company is closing down, the employees thrown out of work, the buildings razed to the ground, the site strewn with salt and then redeveloped as a landfill site processing agricultural by-products? Could you see this as a terrific opportunity to achieve those dreams you mentioned?"

There is, as ever, an element of truth in this particular life coaching attitude to the workplace. Most people in the world are bound by the rules imposed on them by others, in particular by employers. They feel they have to bend and sway in the wind that employment blows, often to such an extent that they develop the habitual twisted stance of the gale-beset tree on the bleak northern hillside. So they re-arrange their priorities to meet their employment demands, instead of re-arranging their employment to suit the lives they want to lead.

> **❝ People feel they have to bend and sway in the wind that employment blows, often to such an extent that they develop the habitual twisted stance of the gale-beset tree. ❞**

There is, the bluffer will point out, 'a balance'.

The trick therefore, that they need to perfect is to find the balance that will keep them in funds, feeling secure, and developing as individuals, while at the same time allowing their employers to feel that the arrangement is equitable.

In terms of the coachee, bringing a rag bag of work problems to the session then, the life coach will seek to move them from (what the coach almost inevitably sees as) a slavering dependence on their employment, towards (what the coach almost inevitably sees as) a more equitable balance of employment and their personal goals. Indeed, the life coach is a paradigm of the now fashionable term 'work-life balance'. The difference is that in the case of life coaches, they own the scales and the weights of work-life balance, while in the case of most of their coachees, the scales and weights are usually owned by the employer, and chained and locked to the employees' legs. The life coach has to persuade coachees (or as bluffers will remind their audience, "help coachees to persuade themselves") that although they may not have realised it, they also have the key to the lock and chain

> **66 To the life coach, all possible threats are capable of being defused or resolved. 99**

'But I'll lose my job!' the coachee may wail. This, as the seasoned bluffer will now realise, is an opener, almost a plea, for further processes. "Are you sure about that?", is the life coach response, followed perhaps by "Have you thought about the alternative possibilities?" and "Would that necessarily be a bad thing?"

To the life coach, all possible threats are capable of being defused or resolved and the only thing that stops anyone from doing so is uncomprehending fear of the consequences.

Hence, 'Would it be so bad to lose your job; after all, you say you hate it' is a perfectly sensible life coach question, even if it is one that coachees could never have dreamed of asking themselves. As so often in the life coaching process, it is the function of life coaches to help their coachees formulate questions about their lives that they should not be afraid to ask and answer. Even if, in life coach terms, the big questions they personally face might be more on the lines of whether to replenish supplies with the Arabic or the Kenyan coffee.

Motivation

It is unlikely that all life coaches will agree with the proposition that they don't actually do anything for their coachees. Nonetheless, if one compares the life coaching deal to the bargain struck with an optician, there is a big difference in what is actually done. For example, both will welcome their coachees in, make them feel at ease, and then use a variety of tests and methods to discover what is wrong. Both will then probably inform the customer what is 'wrong'. But there the similarities cease.

> **❝ 'Would it be so bad to lose your job; after all, you say you hate it' is a perfectly sensible life coach question. ❞**

For while the optician will go on to suggest a

number of things that the optician can do to remedy the situation, the life coach will ask what the customer thinks he or she can do to sort out their problems and then nod sagely. Nodding sagely is what the life coach does. Unlike the optician, with the life coach there is no conversion of the discovered needs into a solution that the coach can supply. No contact lenses, no designer frames, no special solutions, no insurance, no regular check-ups. No 'doing'.

In life coaching it is the customer (coachee) who does the doing. That is the deal. The life coach doesn't even tell the would-be doer what to do, the life coach nods sagely while the coachee works that out for him- or herself.

> **66 In life coaching it is the customer who does the doing. That is the deal. 99**

But the life coach still needs to find some way to ensure that coachees will feel they have achieved something. That is where the motivation comes in. For coachees to do something, they need to be motivated to do it.

It is vital therefore, to find out what the motivation levers are, the ones that will get coachees going, and not just sitting there wallowing in their discomfort. Having found out what it is they are so dissatisfied about, and worked out the ways forward, they still need something to get them to take action. That something, that motivation, is the special ingredient, the seasoning, that the life coach sprinkles over the coachees before they leave, to make sure that when they return they feel satisfied that something has been done, achieved even.

Most people respond to one of two motivation techniques, 'Pull' and 'Push'. It is simplistic to characterise these as 'carrot' and 'stick'. Yet, the bluffer will point out, a substantial carrot wielded properly and with vigour will have much the same effect on the anatomy as a stick, and a stick held out to a drowning man is as attractive as a carrot in a less aquatically challenging situation. (Assuming the drowning man is hungry. And likes carrots.)

> **❝ A substantial carrot wielded properly and with vigour will have much the same effect on the anatomy as a stick, and a stick held out to a drowning man is as attractive as a carrot. ❞**

Pull

Pull motivation is the sort of leverage that creates a situation in coachees' minds that they need to move towards something desirable. So the life coach will help the coachee to work out what his or her vision is, to prepare to bask in the golden glow that it promises, and to realise that moving towards it, even by very small, tentative steps, is the thing the coachee wants to do most in all the world. This achieved, he/she will bound out of the life coach's presence and go off to do something about it before the next session.

Push

Push motivation is a trickier proposition, because it depends on obliging – almost forcing – coachees to get out of the situation they are in. The life coach obviously lacks the conventional instruments for this, like sticks and cattle prods, since a coachee who has been soundly beaten and shocked is unlikely to come back for more.

> **❝ Push motivation is a trickier proposition, because it depends on obliging – almost forcing – coachees to get out of the situation they are in. ❞**

In a nutshell, a life coach employing this form of motivation will be creating some degree of dissatisfaction at the end of each session to spur coachees towards their future or away from their past. Dissatisfaction, the life coach will explain, is at least an improvement on not realising that they ought to be dissatisfied. And of course, if they weren't dissatisfied, why would they have come to the life coach to start with? The logic is inescapable.

Money worries

Happily the life coaching philosophy of non-intervention excludes any and all advice giving, so it would be inappropriate to even ask a life coach for advice on money worries. Since money worries are a prime concern of clients, this comes as quite a relief. Nevertheless, as money is going to be a feature of the coachee's decision making processes, it will keep cropping up. This will happen, especially early on, when coachees are trying to frame the future they want for themselves, or later while trying to set the long term goals that they feel are appropriate to the better life they wish to lead.

> **66** There are always two, and only two, solutions to money problems: to obtain more money, or to dispose of less money. **99**

Life coaches are not at a complete loss when it comes to helping coachees explore the money problems they face. They have at their disposal a very powerful mantra, one that will always take their coachees forward. This is that there are always two, and only two, solutions to money problems;

1 to obtain more money, or
2 to dispose of less.

("Or", the bluffer will say, archly anticipating his audience's inevitable remark, "Do both". Which is not actually a third solution.)

It is far more profitable for the life coach to focus on the side of the equation represented by 'dispose of less money' than to work on the side of 'obtain more money'. This is in part because the matter of obtaining more money can be closely related to the world of work, and there is a whole viper's nest of other issues surrounding work and its monetary or other rewards that confuse the resolution of the essential money-happiness equation.

66 It is far more profitable for the life coach to focus on the side of the equation represented by 'dispose of less money'. 99

Either of the two routes proposed to solve the money-happiness equation is reasonably valid, but the 'dispose of less' route is faster to take. The literature of the world abounds in tales of 'We wuz poor but we wuz happy' families, and there are likewise countless examples of the miserable wealthy (pseudo-clinically referred to as suffering from 'affluenza'). The key to this is that money has first of all to be disassociated from happiness in an individual's mind. This is a challenge that can be met by a series of ('deeply penetrating') questions based initially on the hypothesis that a person doesn't actually need his car/sound system/plasma TV/health club subscription at all.

Initially each suggestion of sacrifice (or rather, each question framed as "Why can't you stop spending your money on….?") will be met with cries of 'But I couldn't possibly give up my …!' by coachees, who, ironically, may well be with the life coach partly because they have the sort of limiting belief typified by 'But I couldn't give up ...'

The life coach then steers coachees though the process of happiness finding by training them to ask themselves 'Why?' they couldn't 'give up' their... Soon they will arrive at the point where they realise that maybe their outgoings are not actually necessary to their happiness, may in fact even be a major cause of misery, and that far from 'giving them up', they could regard their disposal as a much to be desired outcome. When enough of the unwanted expenditures have been curtailed, the coachee reaches the point where he/she has more than enough money for happiness, and even, it is to be hoped, to pay the life coach's fees. With glee.

In a sense, the issue of coachees and their money typifies the whole philosophy of life coaching. There is no point in dwelling on how the situation

> **❝In a sense, the issue of coachees and their money typifies the whole philosophy of life coaching. ❞**

arose, because it is a fact. There is little prospect of the solution appearing as a gift from the gods (lottery wins not being a particularly reliable strategy for balancing the money-happiness equation) but there is a way of resolving the discomfort by the coachees themselves immediately addressing the matter. All that is needed is for the potential consequences of any action to be grasped, understood properly, and accepted. It is not for the world to solve, it is for the coachee to solve. Which is why personal money worries are a quintessential life-coaching specialism.

> **66 It is not for the world to solve, it is for the coachee to solve. 99**

And oddly, one of the easiest to specialise in, being based as it is solely on the exquisitely simple formula of the 'dispose of less or obtain more' kind.

Managing time

As Groucho Marx might have said, (but once again, didn't), "I keep meaning to do something about my time wasting, but never seem to get around to doing it!"

Time management is one of the staples of the life coach's portfolio. This is because it is a need so readily associated with a series of undeniable yet homely propositions that can be easily applied to a coachee's life, such as:

- Your greatest resource is your time

- Lost time is never found again

- Time is the most valuable thing a person can spend.

• Take care in your minutes, and the hours will take care of themselves

At the first hint of an 'issue' (life coaches quite like the word 'issues' because it is less loaded with blame than 'problems' and easier for the coachee to accept) about time and its management, they will have the famous Albert Einstein comparison to hand, that although sitting next to a pretty girl for an hour feels like a minute, placing one's hand on a hot stove for a minute feels like an hour. In addition, time and 'its use' (for 'managing' time is as impossible as knitting fog) provides numerous opportunities for all those meaningful exploratory questions life coaches love, like:

> **66** They will have the famous Einstein comparison to hand, that although sitting next to a pretty girl for an hour feels like a minute, placing one's hand on a hot stove for a minute feels like an hour. **99**

"If you didn't spend your time doing that, how would you spend it?" or,

"What are the things you would most like to stop doing with your time"

Time Management itself itself – the bluffer will wearily admit that the term is now too established to be replaced centres on the essential differences between 'urgent' and 'important' and both of these provide paid-for exploration time in the consultation. For example, getting children into the right school at various stages of education is important, but getting them to school each day is almost inevitably urgent.

> **66 The life coachee will need to be helped to separate and address the urgent before the merely important. 99**

All relationships between important and urgent change as time passes. The life coachee will need to be helped to separate and address the urgent before the merely important, and warned not to spend so much time separating these two categories of activities that suddenly everything becomes urgent.

The life coach will be attempting to ensure that such an unfortunate coalescence of urgent and important does not happen while their coachee is still paying for the consultations. However. if such a thing should happen during consultations on other matters, it can be referred to as 'a bit of a lapse' and may well provide a repeat business opportunity for the coach.

> **66 A good proportion of the day's fee can be earned while one's coachees are mulling over the question of whether decorating the spare room is either urgent or important. 99**

So another advantage for the coach helping coachees plan how to spend their time is that the process consumes even more consultation time. A good proportion of the day's fee can be earned while one's coachees are mulling over the question of whether decorating the spare room is either urgent or important, or is perhaps neither, depending on the goals they have been helped to set for themselves. So a useful question to throw in when discussing time useage is always, "And how does that fit into the goals you have set for yourself?".

> **66** A useful question to throw in when discussing time useage is always, "And how does that fit into the goals you have set for yourself?" **99**

Life coaches will often help the coachees to sort out their time allocation by using the coach's own preferred system, one of which is classification of time spending. In this, coachees are encouraged to develop a list of the things they do with time, and inspect each in terms of a number of different categories suggested by the coach such as:

a **Preparation time** – time spent in the bath, time dressing, commuting, and activities that have to be done to enable other things to happen.

b **Working time** – the time that is exchanged each day for the income needed to support the coachee and dependents.

c **Play time** – the time set aside for activities such as sports, hobbies, or walking the dog.

The bluffer will point out that no single system of time classification is universal because each coachee will vary in the way they use time or the way they interpret that use. So the author or scientist may have 'thinking time' which looks like walking the dog time, or the stressed executive may have 'down time' doing nothing but letting their brain recover from the stresses of the day, although they appear to be watching mindless TV.

> **The author or scientist may have 'thinking time' which looks like walking the dog time.**

In support of this theory of interpreting time use, the expert bluffer will also remember and quote that famous caption from *Punch* magazine to illustrate this, 'Sometimes I sits and thinks, and then again sometimes I just sits.'

But, for the life coach perhaps the most important aspect of time management is ensuring that the consultation runs almost exactly to time. This necessitates the skilful bundling of a coachee's concerns into a package that can be dealt with in precisely the time allocated, without appearing to cut short any but the most obvious verbal ramblings of their coachee, who is after all, paying to use the time of the life coach.

> **For the life coach perhaps the most important aspect of time management is ensuring that the consultation runs almost exactly to time.**

LIFE COACHES' SPECIALISMS

Life coaching seems a rather nebulous occupation. On the one hand it appears to be cover everything, like an unexpected mist on a summer's morning, and on the other hand it isn't easy to see what it actually is, and still less easy to get a grip on it.

As any good business person will tell you, approaching the market with a message that is essentially 'We can do anything, tell us what you want' is a very bad basis for acquiring customers. For while the customer is famously always right (even when they are patently not), the customer is also incredibly indecisive. Like a child at the pick and mix candy counter, dithering and indecision becomes the dominant behaviour. The choice is simply too vast.

❝Like a child with money in hand and an empty bag at the pick and mix candy counter, dithering and indecision becomes the dominant behaviour. ❞

So most life coaches start from a proposition that they can cure you of everything (for which, of course by now you will read as 'will help you to cure yourself of everything') it is a good idea to suggest to potential customers what 'everything' might include. Life coaches tend to specialise, or offer a menu. They hope that, like the customer in the Chinese restaurant, they will choose a main course and then say, 'Oooh! And how about a little plate of number 47 as well!'. (The analogy is not of course precise, because with life coaching once coachees have grasped the general principle and style, or, if you like, worked through the main menu item, they will be quite capable of exploring other items for themselves, and won't need the chef to help them at all.

> **66 With life coaching once coachees have grasped the general principle and style, they will be quite capable of exploring other items for themselves. 99**

So, many life coaches segment their offerings into 'business' and 'personal'. The business side is often dressed up as executive coaching, and offers to help the busy 'executive' – an American use of a word that really just means a person who does what they are told to do – to be a better executive, through clearer thinking, better decision making, and improved personal relationships.

Astute bluffers will notice already that 'clearer thinking, better decision making, and improved personal relationships' looks pretty much like the whole package of life coaching benefits, and they would be right. The difference between the 'Executive life coach' and the 'Personal life coach' is that the executive life coach really does need to have, or convey, some idea of what the world of business is all about, and should ideally have 'been

54

there, done that, got the T-shirt, and made the video. The dedicated personal life coach on the other hand really doesn't need to know anything about the coachee's work situation. In the personal life coaching domains therefore, life coaches over the years have developed a number of specialisms. These include family and parenting, finance, career, and the vaguely named 'personal wellbeing' (mainly a specialism of the more open-toed new age life coach, who may be on a mission to increase the consumption of green tea or promote pyramid based healing).

> **❝ Life coaches over the years have developed a number of specialisms including the vaguely named 'personal wellbeing' (mainly a specialism of the more open-toed new age life coach). ❞**

The point about specialised life coaches is that they should, the coachee thinks, be accustomed to dealing with the type of problems they are presented with. The coachee driven mad by overdrafts, spendthrift children, a crippling mortgage and an expensive golf habit may turn to the life coach offering specialist knowledge and experience in this financial field.

'But what,' the expert will now ask aloud, 'is wrong with that proposition?' Here the master bluffer will pause to fix his audience with a beady eye. And if someone else doesn't do so first, will refer them to the essential absurdity; that the life coach doesn't actually need, nor is it desirable for the life coach to have, any knowledge at all about the problems brought by the coachee. How else can the life coach ask the right questions – the ones that make coachees do the work of thinking the issues through for themselves? If the coach knows about something the coachee is concerned with, there is a danger that he or she will begin to act as a mentor, a person who actually helps with advice and suggestions. And that, you will point out again, is very definitely not what life coaches do.

The life coaching session

There are no fixed lengths for life coaching session, but there are a few guidelines. For example, most coaches will make the point that the first session – they will nearly always say 'first' rather than 'trial', as 'first' carries with it the almost inevitable conclusion that there well be a second, third, and so on – will be longer than usual. This is because the first session needs to set up the basic understanding of the coachee, the situation they want to address, and the commitment they bring to the

> **" Life coaches will nearly always say 'first' session rather than 'trial', as 'first' carries with it the almost inevitable conclusion that there well be a second, third, and so on. "**

process. It also acts as familiarisation for the coach who needs to get used to the sort of ways coachees express themselves, their voices, their mannerisms, and their levels of endurance.

After the first session the following sessions may well drop back to a shorter length, although they will most likely be between 40 and 60 minutes. Life coaches don't like to give the impression that they are watching the clock, and unlike solicitors do not charge by the minute. However there is a certain amount that needs to be covered each session to actually make the process work, and to an extent this must determine the length of the session.

> **"When I last saw you", the coach will say, "you were going to get your lawnmower back from your neighbour who you haven't spoken to for seven years. How did that go?"**

So, for example, the first thing will be the niceties. Getting coachees in through the door, getting them settled, remarking on the traffic, all take time and time is money (the bluffer will point out that in this case it is money for the coach).

Following these niceties the life coach will get right into a 'review'. "When I last saw you", the coach will say, "you were going to get your lawnmower back from your neighbour who you haven't spoken to for seven years. How did that go?" This process of reviewing the events since the last session may well take some time, depending on the complexity of the contributory goal (to get the lawnmower back) the outcomes, and the success (or otherwise of those efforts.

From this part of the session, which should take the meeting up to about the one-third point, the life coach will have drawn out some "issues for today". Cleverly, these will be focussed on the reasons for the success or apparent 'lack of success' (coaches don't like 'failure') or the degree to which the coachee feels the achievement or lack of achievement has taken them.

> **Accomplished life coaches will reach the reinforcement point with about three minutes to spare for the niceties of farewell.**

This will lead into the exploration of the Big Picture, how things have changed in the mind of the coachee, how the pieces of his/her success is emerging, what changes have occurred in his/her thought processes or determination since the last cliffhanger episode of his/her story so far.

This middle section leads into the final part of the session, which is setting the goals for next time, identifying what the snags might be, and determining (that is letting the coachee determine) some ways of overcoming these. Accomplished life coaches will reach the reinforcement point ("So, when I see you next time you are going to tell me that you have put the house on the market!" with about three minutes to spare for the niceties of farewell.

Of course if the coach is working by telephone or (the bluffer can shudder here) by internet, the sessions will be shaped different- ly, and usually take less time. A telephone call of 30 minutes, although wildly popular with teenage girls, is about as much as the coach or the coachee can take

> **66 A telephone call of some 30 minutes, is about as much as the coach or the coachee can take. 99**

without the relief of visual stimulus, and can't contain many of those meaningful pauses that force the coachee to actually answer the question out of, if necessary, sheer embarrassment at the silence otherwise.

Many life coaches, aware of the difficulty that people have in understanding what they do, will also offer an 'introductory session'. These sessions will take a different shape, since:

a) the life coach will do more of the talking, and,
b) there are no real goals to review or set, without benefit of contract.

An introductory session will seldom be as long as a 'proper session', because until the potential coachee signs up, it isn't going anywhere. When the life coach gets a buying or signing up signal from any newcomers, it is possible to propose some suggestions about what they will do next time. Until then it is a bit like a five hour stopover in an exotic airport – too long to spend looking around the airport, but not long enough to go anywhere interesting.

LIFE COACHING QUALIFICATIONS

Finding a good life coach is quite unlike finding someone to instal your gas cooker. Or finding someone to fix your teeth. Quite unlike those quests.

> **"Finding a good life coach is quite unlike finding someone to instal your gas cooker. Or finding someone to fix your teeth."**

If you wish to consult a dentist, it is probable that the person you find, however bad their halitosis, or out-of-date their magazine selection, would not be there on the high street unless they had a qualification, one that is recognised by the government.

It is also highly probable that, as with doctors, should they make a terrible mistake, there are sanctions. In some cases, in order to practise, they also need to be members of a recognised association such as the Confederation of Registered Gas Installers. Obviously, you wouldn't be going to a CORGI member for your dental work, but the principal is the same. Without membership, of the gas installers, the College of Medicine, or another august body, the professional cannot practise.

That's why such doctors, dentists, and gas installers are proud of the certificates they have; they are not just statements of the training they have done, but they are a 'licence to trade', and can be withdrawn, making them effectively unemployable.

So what, the ingénue may ask, about all those certificates that you see behind the reception desk in hotels? Are all those staff members of a professional body too? If I don't get my copy of the *Times* and two soft-boiled eggs in the morning, I can take steps, get redress in some way?

> **66 Certificates don't actually guarantee anything. They are, in short, pretty useless as any sort of protection. 99**

Well, no. All those certificates tell you is that the person concerned has passed a training course of some sort. But such certificates don't actually guarantee anything. They are in short, pretty useless as any sort of protection.

This is where you as sophomore bluffer will say, "And that's more or less the picture with life coaches".

Fancy letters

Many life coaches will boast certificates on their walls. Others will have strings of letters after their names showing how many associations or institutes they belong to, including 'Master Practitioner of the Independent Council of Life Coaches'. But this doesn't tell you that they have a 'licence'. It doesn't give would-be coachees any form of redress should their life coach subsequently prove to need more help than the coachee does.

But surely, a potential coaching customer will ask, if a member of the Honorable Independent Coach Underwriters and Promotion Society (HICUPS) makes a mess of my life, there is something I can do about it? Can't I ask the Independent Council of Life Coaches to drum that useless life coach out of business?

> **It doesn't give would-be coachees any form of redress should their life coach subsequently prove to need more help than the coachee does.**

Well, no. Not even probably. Most such Institutes and Associations are based either on collecting subscriptions or providing training to would-be life coaches. This means they make their money by selling training courses, assessments, and certificates conferring membership. They have no real interest in actually regulating their members. True, they may have all sorts of 'Codes of Conduct' for their members but (as Captain Barbossa put it so elegantly and so devastatingly when a victim invoked the Pirate code, 'And secondly, you must be a pirate for the pirate's code to apply and you are not. And thirdly, the code is more what you'd call 'guidelines' than actual rules!'

As one such body proudly remarks, Life Coaching is, 'An unregulated profession, regulated by our clients.' By 'clients', they mean the people who pay them money to be regarded as the regulators of (how shall we put it?), "regulators of themselves". In a nutshell, all the letters after the life coach's name and all the certificates on the wall promise next to nothing other than that he or she may have been assiduous in their acquisition of qualifications that may or may not be recognised by any 'official' body.

> **66 As Captain Barbossa put it so devastatingly when a victim invoked the Pirate code, 'And secondly, you must be a pirate for the pirate's code to apply. 99**

The best way to choose a life coach, regardless of their certificates and letters, is by personal recommendation from someone you trust. Failing that, select a coach by talking to several, and discovering if (a) any are the sort of person you would feel comfortable talking to, and (b) any are the sort of person you would feel comfortable paying money to for the assumed benefit of talking.

WHERE COACHES COACH

Life coaching has, one might say (the wise bluffer here stressing the 'might', as insurance against ruffled feathers among the listeners), something in common with those improbable get-rich-or-at-least-solvent-quick schemes one sees advertised on placards by motorway roundabouts, or tied illicitly to traffic-lights. Pausing only for a sip of wine, the bluffer elucidates the theory.

> **❝ As a start-up business, life coaching is nearly unique. Unlike a dentist, one doesn't need a surgery (or as has been pointed out, much in the way of qualifications). ❞**

What all those schemes have in common is a promise that by working from home, with hours to suit oneself, the needy and diligent worker can earn large quantities of cash with relatively little effort. In fact, as any bluffer of the world knows full well, the traffic-light placard schemes involve the poor coach paying for the privilege of performing a piffling process more than 24 hours a day just to make a tenth of the figure in the big red font on the sign. But there is for all that a common factor shared with life coaching as a career, and this is that along with the control over working hours, the life coach has a degree of flexibility as to where to work.

As a start-up business, life coaching is nearly

unique. Unlike a dentist, one doesn't need a surgery (or as has been pointed out, much in the way of qualifications). A freelance surveyor presumably needs free lances to practise on, a plasterer needs a radio tuned to a middle-of-the-road radio station, and even the humble hack needs a keyboard to hurriedly hammer out his heartfelt homilies. But the life coach needs nothing really, except (and here the bluffer will do that thing with the stem of the spectacles that makes for a symbol of erudition, for which reason a pair is always carried even if the eyesight does not require them) charm and good listening skills.

Most people, when offered the chance to 'work from home' as it is wont to be called, leap at the chance. They buy themselves a Swedish self-assembly desk, get an upgraded telephone and internet service, and borrow the space by the French windows as 'Mum's' (or 'Dad's') working area. Which is

> **66 The humble hack needs a keyboard to hurriedly hammer out his heartfelt homilies. But the life coach needs nothing really except charm and good listening skills. 99**

just fine, because the children are out of the house by 8.30 for school, the spouse is gainfully employed a short commute away, coffee is freely available all day without the tiresome necessity of speaking to that man from purchasing, and even the dog takes on a whole new dimension as the only living thing who can hear the 'home worker' directing industrial language at their computer. Some home workers even, it has been rumoured, spend all day in scruffy jeans, and don't even shave. Especially the men.

But the problem for the home working life-coach is that to make the work work, the life coaches and their coachees really need to be together in some way, and the sitting room sofa with the smell of old Labrador isn't conducive to the workings of life coaching. Also, it necessitates removing any old beer cans from the windowsill and ensuring that there are no obvious signs of an unordered life, which would be like a driving instructor having a car with obvious signs a recent collision.

> **❝ It necessitates removing any old beer cans from the windowsill and ensuring that there are no obvious signs of an unordered life. ❞**

Even if there is a home office rather than the lounge, a space perhaps formerly occupied by a child and now freed up for less expensive use, the coachee has to be taken there. Is it, for example, upstairs and past the open bathroom and bedroom doors? Will it involve keeping parts of the house especially clean on Mondays and Wednesdays? Is that curry smell from last night capable of removal? All in all, working from home for the life coach is a difficult decision to make, and one that involves, like it or not, the whole family. And possibly the services of a good and regular cleaner.

So other solutions are required to the problem of coaching space, and an immediately obvious solution is an office away from home. But this requires investment, and that normally puts it out of range of the tyro life coach. An office, is not in any case, necessarily ideal for life coaching. While no couch is required in the fine tradition of all those psychiatrist cartoons, a large desk or a conference table is not ideal.

> **66 Nor is an hotel room advisable, for the same reason most reputable hotels don't rent out their rooms by the hour. 99**

Nor is an hotel room advisable, for the same reason most reputable hotels don't rent out their rooms by the hour. (The bluffer will at this point milk the amusement on at least a few of the faces in his or her vicinity).

All of which is why so many coaches turn to two alternative solutions, the house call and the telephone call.

1 The house call

For many coaches this is ideal. In addition to transferring the guilt over that stain on the carpet to the coachee, and leaving it to the coachee to maintain a suitable environment, free of cat fur and such allergens, paying a house call has the advantage of giving the coach an immediate insight into the coachee's seedy past. The bullfight poster in the hallway, the spoof Florida licence plate proudly displayed over the kitchen door, the empty but ornate Italian Strega bottle on the mantelpiece, the pale area where a picture used to hang. All valuable insights which the life coach will notice, tuck away in the back of the mind, and produce with a flourish at some stage when an illustration of insight, empathy, understanding is needed.

> **66 Paying a house call has the advantage of giving the coach an immediate insight into the coachee's seedy past. 99**

House calls also have the advantage of time control. While it is very difficult to escort a sobbing coachee from the coach's own house and into their car in full view of the neighbours, it is a lot easier for the life coach to announce on arriving, "I'm sorry, I really have to keep to time today because I have to be in Luton for six!", and exit when the hour is up. Not necessarily to go to Luton.

2 The telephone call

A new phenomenon has been the growth of an alternative solution, so-called (the bluffer pauses) telephone coaching. This is a very specialised technique for it requires the coach to be fully attentive, making listening noises at quite regular intervals, and coachees to be able to speak confidentially and frankly to a lump of moulded hydrocarbon containing an electromagnetic coil for up to 30 minutes, on their own telephone bill, without eye contact or other non vocal support.

The bluffer will roll the words 'non vocal support' around the mouth (a strong Scottish accent is best for this) to extract the full flavour, and add that this expression refers to all the little signs and indications other than the words used that tell the listener (the life coach) so much about the speaker (the coachee).

> **❝Telephone coaching is a very specialised technique for it requires the coach to be fully attentive... and coachees to be able to speak confidentially and frankly to a lump of moulded hydrocarbon.❞**

Having so pronounced, you are free to warm to the theme of the absurdity of conducting a personal relationship so reliant on empathy while several – possibly hundreds – of miles apart, joined only by fibre optics, and with all the privacy and secrecy of a cell phone conversation on a train.

The bluffer doesn't think much of telephone life coaching, and lets this be known. If pressed, the house call approach will be advised, pointing out that this does have one small disadvantage; nowhere to hang the array of one's certificates, collected from apparently serious, even prestigious life coaching institutes, about which until this point the coachee and his or her entire family, workplace, village or county were blissfully unaware.

THIS AND THAT

Confidentiality

All coaches make a big point of confidentiality. It is, after all, a confidential relationship between coachee and coach. Or should be. Coachees may tell a life coach things about themselves, their family, job, relations and relationships, that they would not like to get out and about. That a coach will refrain from bruiting abroad the information he or she acquires is a reasonable expectation.

> **66 That a coach will refrain from bruiting abroad the information he or she acquires is a reasonable expectation. 99**

There are many professions in the world where confidentiality is protected in various ways. The relationship of doctors to their patient is built on confidentiality, and they will regularly go to the barricades to protect this relationship from intrusion by police, government, or commercial organisations. The solicitor has rights as well as obligations to protect the content of exchanges between themselves and their clients, although from time to time even the most diligent of solicitors will come under pressure from a Judge or politician to break that bond.

Other lesser confidential relationships are such as with a bank manager, but these tend to be based on something called a duty of care, or even more specifically, on various pieces of legislation that prevent personal information being passed to

❝If a bulky policeman is hammering on the life coach's door demanding answers, the cat will in all probability, be well and truly let out of the bag.❞

third parties. Journalists feel very strongly about confidentiality and will from time to time go to prison rather than reveal their sources.

Life coaches have no legal duty of confidentiality, no data protection restriction on the conversations they have with their coachees. Several of the associations and institutes have in their codes of conduct good words about respecting confidences, not revealing conversations, and so on, but if a bulky policeman is hammering on the life coach's door demanding answers, the cat will in all probability, be well and truly let out of the bag.

In short, coachees have to take the confidentiality of life coaches on trust. But then again, as Graham Green had it, it is impossible to go through life without trust. You can however, go through life without a life coach. "Trust me", the bluffer will add, meaningfully.

The need for life coaching

Life coaching is a business that people take up for all sorts of reasons. They may be adopting the Shavian position, that 'those who can, do, and those who can't, teach', or that they have been dealing with problems all their lives and think they may know how to help other people to do the same. They may just be looking for a way to make money. They may, as so many of the Life Coaching training providers say, be looking for 'a better work-life balance', with hardly any preparation, and the chance to choose their own customers, hours, and charges.

> 66 They may, as so many of the Life Coaching training providers say, be looking for 'a better work-life balance', with hardly any preparation, and the chance to choose their own customers, hours, and charges. 99

Or they may have a new vocation. "Vocation", the bluffer will repeat, "not Vacation".

In ages past there was a widespread social rule that the eldest son inherited the farm, the middle became the soldier or professional, and the youngest entered the Church. Only later did vicaring become a 'vocation', something that people were called to. But the fact that many younger sons were rather forcefully shoved into clerical garb did not mean they didn't become good prelates, or that they weren't a great source of help and comfort to their flock, or that they didn't sincerely believe they were doing good.

> **❝The life coach today is in many ways the confessor, the village elder, the old schoolteacher, the family friend, the grandparent with an ear to listen and a wise word to help. ❞**

For they saw themselves as people, who through the good fortune of training, and experience, and belief, were able to bring something to the wider world that the wider world needed.

So with life coaching. People may enter the business (the bluffer has considerable difficulty with calling it a 'profession') for a range of reasons, but they may also find their way to be really valuable to many people who feel they are lacking something in their lives, and do not, as their forebears did, turn to the church in their times of need.

With a fragmented society, uncertain times and increasing complexity of life, there are many people who have no confidante and therefore feel deserted. Many people need an honest friend. Not to tell them what to do, but to let them work it out for themselves, to understand their choices in life, and the consequences of the choices that have.

We can reasonably argue, and the bluffer does, that the life coach today is in many ways the confessor, the village elder, the old schoolteacher, the family friend, the grandparent with an ear to listen and a wise word to help. That may be so. They are part of a long tradition of non-evaluative listeners, replacing in many people's lives something that has gone missing.

"For all their failings," you can say with conviction, "the world probably needs life coaches."

SO, YOU WANT TO BE A LIFE COACH?

Life coaching is presented as a serious career option, and few could say it is any less serious as a career option than other 'new careers' we have seen develop – in say wedding planning, bouncy castle rental, graffiti artistry, or worm farming. The life coaching spiel is very persuasive and suggestive. It offers the opportunity to set your own hours of work, choose your own customers, set your own income levels, and be your own boss. It is hard, as even the

> **66 Few could say life coaching is any less serious as a career option than say wedding planning or worm farming. 99**

seasoned bluffer will acknowledge, to deny the attractiveness of the package apparently on offer.

But the bluffer will, if asked for an honest evaluation, also try to place the life coaching prospectus into the history of similar offers that have been made to the public from time to time. For example, countless would-be entrepreneurs spent many miserable months trying to sell washing powders and unguents to relatives and friends, simply to pay off the licence they bought for the right to try and sell these essentially expensive and unwanted commodities.

> **66 Look on any life coaching web site, at the back of any life coaching book, and you will note that many of the loudest protagonists of life coaching seem to have a rather obvious double agenda. 99**

Look on any life coaching web site, at the back of any life coaching book, and you will note that many of the loudest protagonists of life coaching seem to have a rather obvious double agenda. On the one hand they are promoting themselves as apparently successful life coaches, while on the other hand they are trying to market themselves as consultants on life coaching, or as trainers of would-be life coaches. It seems to the bluffer, who has been around for a while, uncomfortably like a 'pyramid selling scheme', one of those arrangements where the real money is made by licensing the right to sell, rather than by actually selling anything.

So before embarking on life coaching as a future career, it is essential to ask oneself a few questions, such as 'What will it cost me?' and 'Who can I really learn from?'. There are also a number of 'what if?' questions, such as 'What if no-one else feels remotely inclined to consult me?' or 'What if the whole 'life coaching industry' proves to be about as permanently profitable as a hula hoop franchise?'

> **❝ Just as the good life coach asks the questions that invite their coachees to see their own world as it really is, questions help the would-be life coach to face the realities of trying to make a living from it. ❞**

These are, the bluffer points out, hard questions for the person who really wants to work with people by life coaching. But just as the good life coach asks the questions that invite their coachees to see their own world as it really is, and to decide what they want to do about it, these hard questions help the would-be life coach to face the realities of trying to make a living from it.

If the potential life coach decides to proceed, there are a huge number of offers of training and support, and any internet search will reveal many options for learning the trade. Most will promise to develop both life coaching skills and 'the business side'. Of the two, the latter is the bigger trap.

Remember that there have actually been many better mousetraps, and the world is not exactly covered in pathways beaten to their inventors' doors.

Choose the training option that is right for you, also bearing in mind that any certificate or 'qualification' you may achieve purely in life coaching will have almost no value or meaning to your coachees whatsoever. Choose, if possible, a training process that includes not only 'life coaching', but also other more established forms of coaching as well, such as executive or workforce coaching, small business coaching, or even relationship coaching. This will provide a far better chance of making a living from 'coaching' if 'life coaching' doesn't work out.

Make sure also that the time is right. If the future life coach is in the midst of a career, with family obligations, a mortgage, children to support, and a substantial credit card debt, it may not be a good time to tell the bank manager that the previ-

> **66 It may not be a good time to tell the bank manager that the previously regular pay check will be stopping for the sake of following what most bank managers will see as a 'new age fad'. 99**

ously substantial and regular pay check will be stopping for the sake of following what most bank managers will see as a 'new age fad'. Many life coaches find they have to make their 'real money' from other activities, even by going 'back to work' to support what has become their life coaching hobby. Ask yourself if you can do this if it proves necessary.

You will also need, in your own life, the security of knowing that you have a solid emotional base before you can help others, many of whom will inevitably bring their often painful concerns to your doorstep, rather like a cat after a night's hunting will bring its little dismembered gifts to your clean living room carpet.

> **"Many will bring their often painful concerns to your doorstep, rather like a cat after a night's hunting will bring its little dismembered gifts to your clean living room carpet. "**

Look also to the market for the service. What tangible signs are there of a need for life coaching in the local area? Are there any other life coaches making a living (and the bluffer stresses the last three words heavily, pausing for effect, and repeating them) out of life coaching in the area?

Consider, too, how you will market the service. Vendors of life coaching training will talk glibly of 'How to get free publicity' and 'public speaking opportunities' but to be sure, if they were doing this effectively themselves, they would neither be selling life coaching training, nor telling people how to compete with them. It is not easy to get that fabled 'free publicity' (and, the bluffer will add, it is seldom actually free anyway). Offers to speak about life coaching at local groups and events rarely place the life coach in front of people who want to buy the service. Newspaper editors – even local ones – do not beat a path to the coach's door for an article.

This said, if you have done your research, have the messages right, and have an offer of free publicity, grab it. After all, someone will read it, and as Oscar Wilde put it: "There is only one thing worse than being talked about and that is *not* being talked about."

So, you still want to be a life coach?

If you imagine having a rewarding, high paying, flexible job coaching people to achieve success in their lives, their relationships, or their careers, by all means do so. But make sure your decisions are based on the reality of your situation, and a true understanding of the likely results of the actions you take. After all, that's what your life coach would advise.

And the bluffer turns to leave, knowing that behind him/her the audience is silently mouthing to each other, 'But life coaches don't give advice!'

GLOSSARY

Angst A much more impressive word for anxiety. Don't let it worry you.

Closed question A question that invites a 'yes' or 'no' answer, such as 'Did you put the cat out?' Coaches much prefer, 'What do you do with the cat at night?' as the answer to this gives them opportunities to help you to explore all the cat-management options that are actually open to you when you take control of your life.

Comfort zone A feeling that coachees may have that they are more or less happy with the situation they are in, and see no great need to do anything about it. It is a primary objective of the life coach to lever their coachees out of their comfort zone, on the basis that if it is really that nice it must be bad for them, like doughnuts or chips with mayonnaise.

Depression A clinical condition that life coach should not get involved with. Not to be confused with 'depressed', which is a state of mind, and can be addressed by life coaching.

Empathy Understanding why someone feels miserable, even if that doesn't give them any real comfort.

Explore A word that coaches use when they think you are probably deluding yourself by stating positions that no-one else would regard as remotely sensible. When you 'explore' something you take a machete to the jungle of ideas and beliefs that have grown up around you, and discover that there is, after all, a path to be followed. You don't need a coach to help you explore – just start asking what you might do instead of allowing the jungle to grow unimpeded.

Failure Not yet success.

Fatalism A feeling that it really doesn't matter what you do, as your life is not in your control, and what will be, will be, or 'Que sera, sera'. The idea is anathema to life coaches, who may take a dozen sessions to change this attitude in their coachees, by which time the coachees realise that indeed they can take control of events, or could, if only they hadn't spent all their money on coaching.

Feedback A way of filling out the time by going over what has been said twice already, and telling each other that it was really jolly useful and very promising.

Fear of failure A sense of self preservation that prevents people doing foolish things, but is regarded as undesirable by many a life coach as it can also prevent coachees from doing really sensible things, even if they fail in the attempt and then revert to obsessing about being useless. Which means they can be signed up for an extra course of sessions in self-confidence. Or obsession management.

Goals Things it would be quite nice to achieve, and to which you can direct your efforts. As you explore your situation in your coaching relationship, you often realise you were trying to achieve the 'wrong goals', and possibly even playing the wrong sport. Coaches will tell you that they regard this as 'progress'.

Grief cycle A good general purpose way of describing how people react to change, including 'Shock', 'Denial', 'Anger', 'Bargaining' and 'Acceptance'. The only real question is why it is a cycle, as this implies, rather gloomily, that as soon as one gets over one major disaster, there's another one just about to happen.

GROW A popular coaching methodology, standing for Goals, Reality, Options, Wrap-up. Coaches need some idea of how to go about their session with you, and GROW is as good a way as any. Another way of putting it might be, 'What are you trying to achieve?', 'What's stopping you?', 'What can you do about it?' and 'When shall I see you again?'

Habit   Something the coachee mistakes for an addiction, like eating chocolate while watching *Desperate Housewives*. Habits can be broken relatively easily, unlike addictions.

I'm OK, You're OK.   Based on the work of Erich Berne, this is a desirable 'ego state' to be in. It's an attitude to life. The other three positions are:
'I'm OK, you're not OK' (Arrogance)
'You're OK, I'm not OK' (Inferiority)
'You're not OK, I'm not OK' (Let's all commit hara-kiri)

Life events   Almost anything that happens to you and has the effect of getting you a bit stressed. If you add up all your life events you find that you have a perfectly rational explanation for why you suddenly started to throw kippers at the cat.

Life purpose   Something you would like people to remember you as having achieved, or if you don't wish to be remembered just yet, the thing you would most like to 'Do With Your Life'.

Limiting belief   In general, any opinion of ourselves that starts with 'I can't' or an analogous opening. Most limiting beliefs are simply lazy nonsense, but can be quite comfortable, see 'comfort zone'.

Listening skills   The stock in trade of the life coach, who relies on listening well, and being seen to listen, to convey the impression that the coachee is unique and special.

Maxim or **mantra**   Intensely annoying, yet somehow deeply meaningful phrases such as 'Everyone can achieve more' and 'A person's past is not an indication of their future'. With enough 'maxims and mantras, you don't need a life coach at all.

Metaphor   A way of describing things using mental pictures, much favoured by coaches. "I want you to regard the next few weeks as your journey to the top of your own personal mountain" is one such. And "along the way you're going to have to leave base camp behind", "carry your load a bit further", and possibly "stand on the summit and look at the world from there".

Money troubles   An inability to balance income against outgoings, which the life coach can help the coachee to address, as long as there is enough in his/her bank account to pay for that help – in which case the client hasn't got money trouble.

Motivation How life coaches get their coachees to decide that they need to 'do something positive' about their life, and then actually get them to do it, all without laying a finger on them.

NLP Neuro Linguistic Programming A set of theories popular with some life coaches, based on the idea that the way you think is linked to the way you behave. Or that the way you behave is linked to the way you think. It's obviously a huge advance in understanding ourselves.

Open question One that gives the life coach a lot of time to frame the next question, such as "What would you like to do?", rather than "Would you like to be rich?" which is a closed question, and gives no thinking time at all.

Principle An absolute statement of something that you believe in, and which you use to help you to make wise and informed decisions. Until a better principle comes along.

Procrastination Either a very sound strategy involving not doing what you don't yet need to do, or a very unsound tendency not to do things that really ought to be done. Take your pick.

Rule Something you are supposed to obey, but don't. Rules are easy to abandon, because they are always devised for now, and 'now' changes. Avoid rules, stick to principles

Stress Good for you if there is just enough in your life; bad for you if there is too much. Like chocolate really. What coachees need in small amounts just to get up in the morning, but if excessive, will cause them to make bad decisions and get rather ratty, even with their life coach.

Therapist Someone who is probably professionally qualified to deal with the results of an illness or injury, so not a life coach.

Time management A quasi-religious belief based on the amazing discovery that a day only has 24 hours. It is essentially about learning that holding conversations with an automated telephone system is a waste of precious time.

Vision Something you can't see, but is supposed to inspire you to change your life.

Whys (five) An intensely irritating rule that coaches use to get to the bottom of things, involving asking "Why?" five times, which if over-used could end with "Why are you looking at me like that?"

THE AUTHOR

George Edwards divides his time between his current job in China and his home in Spain with deceptively effortless disorganisation, a ridiculous work-life balance he has cultivated over what can only loosely be called a career.

Much good luck and consecutive unemployment opportunities have taken him into many well-paid sinecures in the military, oil, electronics, engineering, health and even education sectors, many of which have survived his contributions. At some point he evolved into a genial but fairly wise old fart, and now can earn a living yet avoid responsibility by finding inventive ways to tell young career-climbers the questions to ask themselves instead of the answers they seek, and that "Yes", they can certainly pay for the dinner.

Along the way he has had published over 20 slim volumes on management, training, and self-development, at least one of which is still in print, but only because he published it himself.

At the last count he had thus bluffed his way through some 17 jobs, 12 companies, at least eight occupations, in seven countries, but he has promised himself that next year he will definitely find time to decide what he wants to do when he grows up.

Consultancy

The essence of consultancy is simply stated, and you should never fail to bear it in mind. You are there to do the dirty work. Never suppose for a single moment that any of your careful recommendations will necessarily be put into effect.

Skiing

There is no such thing as a comfortable ski boot; just concentrate on finding one which doesn't make you pray for an early death. The admission of ski boot agony suggests the probability of inexperience. Experts never whinge about their boots.

Doctors

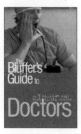

The doctor in casualty is expected to examine, diagnose and treat more patients per hour than the average person serving in McDonald's. At the end of eight hours you feel like walking into moving traffic. The only thing that stops you is the depressing thought that the ambulance would bring you straight back again.

Management

There are several extremely respectable reasons for avoiding decisions without appearing indecisive. The first can be expressed by the following helpful aphorism: 'If change is not necessary, it is very necessary not to change'.

Small Business

Your Business Plan must include a Budget. When it becomes clear that this is completely unrealistic, it can be updated by Forecasts, which in turn can be replaced by 'Revised Forecasts' when they, too, prove to be inaccurate.

The Flight Deck

Airlines like their pilots to make firm landings. The wheels are stationary. The runway is passing by at around 150 mph. The two have to meet up. If the pilot does a smoothie, the tyres drag along the runway surface without spinning up which burns off rubber. A firm landing gets the wheels spinning with less loss of expensive tread.

Comments on other titles

On the series:
"With the vital information from these books there should be no subject upon which you can't give an informed opinion (or at least one that sounds informed.)"

Reviewer, *Aberdeen Evening Express*

Archaeology:
"Unmissable! Indispensable for old and new archaeologists alike, this is a fabulous book. It is one of the few books which made me laugh out loud in a public library."

Reader from Sheffield

Consultancy:
"A great guideline for evaluating consultants. Lots of humor, but also very practical tips for the wannabees."

Reader from Kentucky

Men:
"Irresistible and captivating. Men will find it infuriatingly accurate."

Reader from Santa Barbara

Music:
"Hobnob with the critics. Everything you need to know with all the right things to say. Extremely witty and well written."

Reader from Los Angeles

the Bluffer's® Guides

Oval Books

*This Bluffer's® Guide is available
as a downloadable audiobook:
www.audible.co.uk/bluffers

We like to hear from our readers.
Please send us your views on our books
and we will publish them as appropriate on
our web site: ovalbooks.com.

Oval Books also publish the best-selling
Xenophobe's® Guide series –
see www.ovalbooks.com

Both series can be bought via Amazon or directly
from us, Oval Books through our web site
www.ovalbooks.com or by contacting us.

Oval Books charges the full cover price
for its books (because they're worth it) and
£2.00 for postage and packing on the first
book. Buy a second book or more and postage
and packing will be entirely FREE.

To order by post please fill out the accompanying
order form and send to:

Oval Books
5 St John's Buildings
Canterbury Crescent
London SW9 7QH

cheques should be made payable to: Oval Books

or phone us on +44 (0)20 7733 8585
or visit our web site at: www.ovalbooks.com

Payment may be made by Visa or Mastercard and orders are
dispatched as soon as the card details and mailing address are
received. If the mailing address is not the same as the card holder's
address it is necessary to give both.

Oval Books